CW01459548

Table of Contents

Welcome to Pembrokeshire! 7
    Overview 7
    Culture...8
    Location & Orientation 9
    Climate & When to Visit.......................................10

Sightseeing Highlights 12
    Pembroke 12
    Pembroke Castle 13
    St Davids..13
    St Davids Cathedral 14
    Dr Beynon's Bug Farm 15
    Tenby...16
    Tudor Merchant's House 17
    Carew Castle...17
    Manorbier Castle 18
    Caldey Island 19
    Folly Farm Adventure Park & Zoo 20
    Pembrokeshire Coast National Park 21
    Pembrokeshire Coast Path 21
    Preseli Mountains 22
    Stackpole Estate & Barafundle Bay 23
    St Govan's Chapel 24
    Skomer Island...24
    St Dogmaels 25
    Teifi Marsh Nature Reserve.................................26
    Amroth 26
    Fishguard..27
    The Last Invasion Tapestry Gallery.......................27
    Haverfordwest 28
    Picton Castle 28
    Oakwood Theme Park...29
    Blue Lagoon Water Park......................................30
    Milford Haven 30
    Dyfed Shire Horse Farm 31

Recommendations for the Budget Traveller 33
    Places to Stay...33
        The County Hotel 33

Pembrokeshire Travel Guide

Sightseeing, Hotel, Restaurant & Shopping Highlights

Samantha Jones

White Rose Guest House..34
Lakeland Guesthouse 34
Seaview Hotel 35
Farmstays in Pembrokeshire..35
Places to Eat..**37**
The Sound Cafe 37
Ocean Restaurant 37
Tenby's Fish & Chips Restaurant..38
Wavecrest Cafe..38
The Georges Restaurant & Cafe Bar 39
Places to Shop **40**
The Sheep Shop 40
Wickedly Welsh Chocolate..40
The Nook..41
Felin Fach Handmade Textiles..41
Shopping in Narberth 42

Welcome to Pembrokeshire!

Overview

Pembrokeshire in the south western region of Wales is rightly famous for its attractive, rugged coastline. Rich in natural beauty, it forms part of the Pembrokeshire Coast National Park, which offers unspoilt beaches, access to remote islands and gorgeous scenery. There are also fascinating insights into early Celtic history.

The Preseli Mountains are believed to be the source for the ancient boulders now situated at Stonehenge and there are several prehistoric burial sites scattered across the region.

The county has two historical religious shrines. St Davids Cathedral, located within the UK's smallest city of St Davids, honours the patron saint of Wales in the area where his original congregation was founded more than a thousand years ago.

Meanwhile St Govan's Chapel fascinates visitors with its unusual location within the crevice of a cliff. Pembrokeshire is also home to several significant Norman castles, including Pembroke Castle, the birthplace of Henry VII. Its strategic location has placed it at the forefront of several attempts to conquer Ireland. Today, the ferry at Pembroke Dock still offers access to Wales' neighbour across the Irish Sea.

Pembrokeshire is home to thousands of Welsh puffins and these marine birds are the county's official emblem. Visit Skomer Island, for one of the largest breeding colonies. Another recommendation for animal lovers is Folly Farm an Adventure Park and Zoo that has been voted the best day out in Wales.

Adrenalin junkies can experience the rush of coasteering, Pembrokeshire's own homegrown extreme sporting activity. Coasteering combines rock-climbing, caving and cliff-jumping.

Culture

The Celtic peoples first settled in Wales during the Iron Age. They refer to themselves as the Cymry, a name that first appears in written language around 633. The Welsh language, also known as Cymreag, belongs to the Brythonic family and is a relative of Breton and the now extinct Cornish.

The earliest surviving examples of Welsh epic poetry dates back to the 6th century and, following the proud tradition of early poets such as Taliesin and Aneirin, poetry and music are still important aspects of Welsh culture.

Dylan Thomas is the best known Welsh poet of more recent times.

Many road signs are given in English and Welsh and Welsh was recognized as an official language by the Welsh Language Act of 1967. A favourite linguistic export of the Welsh is *cwtch*, the Cymreag word for cuddle.

Pembrokeshire was occupied by the Normans from 1100 and is one of the more anglicized counties of Wales. The town of Haverfordwest is sometimes referred to as "Little England". It is in this county that the first Tudor king, Henry VII was born, marking the end of centuries of conflict between English and Welsh rulers.

The Methodist church enjoys the strongest following in Wales, with the Anglican and Roman Catholic Church taking second and third place respectively.

Agriculture and mining are important industries in Wales. The leek is an important ingredient in Welsh cuisine, as well as cheese, which is abundant. Traditional dishes are *laverbread*, a seafood dish and *cawl,* a type of broth. The Really Wild Food Festival in St Davids coincides with the Spring Bank Holiday and the Narberth Food Festival takes place towards the end of September.

Fishguard hosts several annual music festivals, including the Fishguard Folk Festival in May, the International Music Festival in July and a jazz and blues festival in August. The Tenby Blues Festival takes place in November.

Location & Orientation

Pembrokeshire is bordered by the counties of Ceredigion and Carmarthenshire and includes a long, jagged stretch of coastline, punctuated with numerous bays and rocky outcrops. Overall Wales is mountainous and the Preseli Mountains form a prominent spine across the territory of Pembrokeshire. Its commercial and administrative capital is Haverfordwest.

The nearest major airport is at Cardiff which provides connections to various UK destinations, Cork and Dublin in Ireland and to Paris and Amsterdam.

Pembrokeshire is connected by rail to London via Swansea. A ferry service connects Pembrokeshire with Ireland via Pembroke Dock and Fishguard. By road, you can reach Wales from London via the M4 Motorway. A regular coach service connects Pembrokeshire to London, Birmingham and various other destinations in the UK.

The Pembrokeshire Coastal route is covered by a local bus network that runs seven days a week during the summer months (from May to September). This covers the entire coastline from St Dogmaels to Amroth. A reduced service is in effect during the winter months. The Poppit Rocket connects Cardigan with Fishguard via St Dogmaels and Newport. The Strumble Shuttle connects Fishguard to St Davids. The Puffin Shuttle links St Davids with Marloes, which lies just west of Milford Haven. There is also a bus service linking St Davids with Haverfordwest, as well as a service linking Haverfordwest with Dale. There are circular routes around St Davids (the Celtic Coaster) and Pembroke Dock (the Coastal Cruiser). If you are planning to do a fair amount of travelling by bus, consider investing in a West Wales Ranger Ticket, for reduced rates. Dogs are allowed on the service, at the driver's discretion.

Climate & When to Visit

Pembrokeshire enjoys a maritime climate which experiences frequent cloud cover and wind, as well as a fair percentage of rain. Temperatures are relatively mild.

The warmest period is from June to September, with the hottest temperatures occurring in July and August. Day averages for those months are around 19 degrees Celsius, with night temperatures of around 15 degrees Celsius being typical. August is generally the wettest month of the summer period.

Most towns see an average annual rainfall around 880mm, with monthly averages between 92mm and 105mm occurring in the wettest months (October to January) and rainfall around 52mm being typical in the driest months from April to July.

The resort town of Tenby is one of the sunnier places in Wales. Here you see highs of 19.5 degrees Celsius in July and August and temperatures between 7.4 and 2.6 degrees Celsius in January and February. Tenby sees an average monthly rainfall between 91 and 105 in the wettest months, from October to January. Even between April and July, a monthly rainfall between 51 and 57mm is typical. Expect temperatures between 17.9 and 11.5 degrees Celsius in June and September and 14.7 and 8.8 degrees Celsius in May and October.

It is always wise to pack rain gear for a holiday in Pembrokeshire, even when visiting in the summer months, and the cooler weather makes it a great destination for hiking in the county's abundant natural scenery.

The best time to visit for puffin viewing is from May to early July. The chicks generally hatch in June. The summer months are also great for viewing dolphins and whales. In spring, the countryside is adorned with colourful flowers. Birdwatchers viewing the avian migrations will want to book their stay for autumn. Hikers who walk the coastal routes of Pembrokeshire during autumn may also glimpse seal pups on the county's wilder beaches.

Sightseeing Highlights

Pembroke

Pembroke was once the county town of Pembrokeshire. Its history goes back 900 years and one of its most prominent landmarks is Pembroke Castle, the birthplace of Henry VII. Significant portions of its medieval walls are still visible. Near the castle, remnants of Monkton Priory can be found can be found in a few scattered arches and a gable wall. Monkton Old Hall is regarded as one of the oldest domestic buildings in Pembrokeshire.

Get acquainted with recent local history at the Pembroke Dock Heritage Centre. It is located in Pembroke Dock's historical dockyard and you will be able to learn more here about the rigors of shipbuilding and also, the famous Sunderland flying boats of World War Two.

Pembroke Castle

Pembroke, Wales
Tel: 01646681510
http://pembroke-castle.co.uk/

Pembroke Castle is the largest privately owned castle in Wales and played a key role that impacted on various periods of English history. It was first built in 1093, at the dawn of Norman rule in Britain. In the late 12th century, it was given to William Marshall, the first Earl of Pembroke by Richard I. He had served the monarchs of England as a loyal knight for several decades. One of the most significant events in the castle's history was the birth of Henry VII. His mother, Margaret Beaufort, lived at the castle for several years thereafter.

On the free guided tour, you can learn more about the lives of the castle's past inhabitants and enjoy the beautiful scenery from the castle ramparts. The castle regularly hosts events such as falconry displays, battle re-enactments, dragon days and knight schools. It was used as a setting for various films including *The Lion in Winter*, *Jabberwocky* by Terry Gilliam and the 1989 version of *Prince Caspian*. Visitors can purchase postcards, books and other gift items at the castle shop.

St Davids

Originally known as Mynyw, St David was founded around the monastery and church of David. After his death, the site became a shrine attracting many pilgrims, including William the Conqueror and Henry II.

The settlement also occupied a key position where several important land and sea routes intersected, providing access to England, Wales and Ireland. It was conferred with city status in the 16th century but lost it in the 1890s when it fell into decline. Queen Elizabeth II reaffirmed its city status in 1994. St David is the smallest and least populous city in the UK.

St David is located within the Pembrokeshire Coast National Park and offers access to the islands of Skomer, Ramsey, Grassholm and Skokholm. For a mix of nature and art, go to the Oriel y Parc Visitor Centre, where you can learn more about the surrounding landscape and view a collection of art by Graham Sutherland. From the walk towards St David's Head, you will be able to enjoy good sea views of Ramsey Island. The beach is great for surfing.

St Davids Cathedral

St Davids Cathedral has a long history which goes back all the way to the 6th century, making it one of the oldest episcopal sees to be found in Britain. It was founded by Saint David who was the first bishop and is the patron saint of Wales.

From the 7th century until 1097 the church endured numerous Viking raids, but thrived by forging connections with English rulers such as King Alfred of Wessex and William the Conqueror. William visited the church to pray in 1081. Norman rule brought greater stability.

The cathedral is located in a hollow on a hillside, beside the ruins of the bishop's palace. You can pay homage to the mortal remains of its founding father, Saint David, at the crypt.

Other historical figures interred here include Gerald of Wales and Edmund, the Earl of Richmond. One of the more striking features of the interior is the floating altar. The library holds a wealth of manuscripts, some dating back to the 16th century, as well as 19th century photographs of the cathedral. There is also a gorgeous set of stained glass windows. In the cathedral, you will find chapels dedicated to St Thomas Becket and St Edward the Confessor as well as the Holy Trinity Chapel and the Lady Chapel. Visit the Gatehouse for exhibition detailing the cathedral's long history and its role in the world today. Also in this part of the cathedral, you can view the Medieval Bell and the Abraham Stone.

St Davids is an active cathedral with daily services as well as choir practice. No admission is charged, but donations are welcome. To photograph the interior you will need a photography permit for a fee of £2.00. Guided tours can be arranged in English or Welsh.

Dr Beynon's Bug Farm

Lower Harglodd Farm,
St Davids, Pembrokeshire, SA62 6BX
Tel: 07966 956357
http://www.drbeynonsbugfarm.com/

Dr Sarah Beynon's Bug farm is a working research centre dedicated to the study of insects. The main rooms include the Tropical Zoo and the Bug Museum where you can view specimens of various species of insect. If you are not too squeamish, do not miss the handling sessions where you can touch hissing cockroaches, stick insects and larvae. Take a walk through the miniature replica of a farm and learn more about the insects it attracts.

There is a lively calendar of bug-themed events throughout the year. In the Bug Kitchen, you can sample some edible critters - there are cricket cookies and bug burgers - but regular food options are also available. Admission is £6.50. As the bug farm can be quite busy, booking is advised.

Tenby

The picturesque harbour town of Tenby dates back to Norman times and its charming medieval character is still evident in the narrow cobbled streets and remaining city walls. Explore its history by paying a visit to the Tenby Museum and Gallery or 15th century church of St Mary.

Since the Georgian era Tenby has become a popular seaside resort. It has an attractive promenade and its three beaches, South Beach, North Beach and Castle Beach all carry Blue Flag ratings.

The town has two golf courses and various water sport facilities offering kayaks and motorboats for hire. Mackerel fishing trips can be arranged. There is a ferry service to the nearby monastic retreat on Caldey Island. A nightly walking tour will acquaint you with the town's ghost and vampire legends.

Several amusement and theme parks can be visited from Tenby. The Dinosaur Park will appeal to young children, who can meet over 30 replicas of different dinosaurs.

Other attractions include an off-road circuit for kids, a giant Astra slide and trampolining. A range of fun pursuits can be enjoyed at Heatherton World of Activities. There is a hedge maze, a clay shooting range, go-karts, jumping pillows and Crazy Golf.

Have fun with a water balloon battle or visit one of six paintball battle zones. For adventure, tackle the tree tops trail. Admission is free, with a pay as you play system in place.

Tudor Merchant's House

Quay Hill,
Tenby SA70 7BX, Wales
Tel: 01834 842279
https://www.nationaltrust.org.uk/tudor-merchants-house

In the 1500s, the Earl of Pembrokeshire was an influential ally and relative of Henry VII and the area flourished from a thriving sea trade. Today, visitors to the Tudor Merchant's House can enjoy a glimpse into the everyday life of a Tudor merchant. The home is furnished with replicas of Tudor furniture and children will be able to dress up in Tudor costumes and play with Tudor era toys. Wall hangings depict scenes from medieval and Tudor life in Tenby, while informative presentations will acquaint you with the origins of certain popular sayings.

Carew Castle

Castle Lane,
Tenby SA70 8SL, Wales
Tel: 01646 651782

Carew Castle is one of the finest castles in the south of Wales. Its first incarnation – a structure of timber - was built around 1100 by Gerald of Windsor, a Norman who married the welsh Princess Nest and received the site as part of the dowry.

The current castle was built in 1270 by Nicholas de Carew, one of his descendants and it remained in their possession until the turbulent period following the Black Death.

One of the most illustrious events in the history of Carew Castle occurred in 1507, when it had fallen into the ownership of the influential Rhys ap Thomas. He hosted a grand tournament, which was attended by Henry VII, his son Arthur and daughter in law, Catherine of Aragon. To mark the occasion, their coats of arms can still be seen on the porch. Rhys also added the ornate fireplace in the hall. The north wing was added by Sir John Perrot, the bastard son of Henry VIII, who was a later tenant.

Other notable features are the Carew Cross monument near the entrance, the large Tudor-style windows and the surviving 13th century towers. Carew Mill, the only complete tidal mill in Wales, dates back to 1801. It now houses a museum.

Carew Castle is currently administered by the Pembrokeshire Coast National Park. It overlooks the Carew inlet, which forms part of the Milford Haven Waterway.

Archaeological excavation has revealed signs of earlier fortification. Fragments of Roman pottery have also been uncovered.

Daily guided tours are available at 10.30am and 2.30pm and there is a gift shop, as well as a picnic area. Carew Castle periodically hosts re-enactments and other events. Admission is £6. Audio guides are available.

Manorbier Castle

http://manorbiercastle.co.uk/

With its seaside setting, Manorbier Castle is one of the most picturesque Norman castles in Pembrokeshire. It was built during the 12th century by Odo de Barri and its structures have remained relatively well-preserved.

Historical lives are depicted with life-sized wax models in period dress. There is a holiday cottage on the grounds, which can be rented. Manorbier Castle served as a setting for the BBC's production of *The Lion, the Witch and the Wardrobe*. Manorbier Castle is in Manorbier Village, about 8km from Tenby.

Caldey Island

The history of Caldey Island dates back 1500 years. Its first inhabitants were a community of Celtic monks led by the abbot Pyro, also known as Ynys Byr. The first monastery was destroyed by the Vikings, but from the 12th century until 1536, the year of the Dissolution, a Benedictine order flourished here, leaving the ruins of a medieval priory. A new group of Benedictines came in 1906. Bowing to economic pressures, they gave way to the current residents, a group of Cistercians from Belgium.

A 20 minute boat ride from Tenby will take you to the island where you can enjoy its peaceful atmosphere and beautiful scenery.

There are scheduled monastic services at 12.15pm and 2.20pm and you can tour the chocolate factory and the perfume factory. Their wares are available at the gift shop. If you have post cards, get them stamped with a unique Caldey Island stamp at the post office.

Priory Beach offers a secluded sandy beach for swimming or sun bathing. The island also has a lighthouse and a tearoom.

Folly Farm Adventure Park & Zoo

Begelly, Kilgetty SA68 0XA,
Tel: 01834 812731
https://www.folly-farm.co.uk/

Folly Farm Adventure Park and Zoo is located on a former dairy farm in the Welsh countryside and is a 10 minute drive from Saundersfoot.

At Folly Farm you can see a variety of farm and wild animals in habitats that have been adapted to resemble their natural environments. Among the resident animals are lions, monkeys, meerkat, donkeys, giraffes, rhinos, parrots and tortoises.

Scheduled events throughout the day involve close encounters with some of the animals. Meet and greet with a ferret, a guinea pig, a rabbit or a cockroach. Milking time for the goats is at noon and 2.30pm.

Another highlight, penguin feeding time, is at 11am and 2pm. Additionally, you can join the adorable miniature pigs on their daily walk or attend informative talks on rhinos, giraffes, penguins and lions.

While the animals definitely take centre stage, Folly Farm has several other attractions. Cruise the grounds on the land train and see grazing horses, alpacas, llamas, goats, sheep and deer. There is an indoor and outdoor play area, with vintage carousel rides and a go-kart track, as well as several eateries and a picnic area.

Admission costs £13.95. You will need tokens for the fairground and the go-kart track and these cost 50p each.

Penguin feeding and giraffe feeding cost £39 each.

Pembrokeshire Coast National Park

The Pembrokeshire Coast National Park was created in 1952 and offers over 900km of public footpaths and riding trails. Besides the Pembrokeshire Coast National Trail of almost 300km, there are well over 200 circular trails featuring spectacular scenery, unspoilt beaches and an abundance of natural wildlife. For a mobile guide to various sights, activities and upcoming events, download the Coast to Coast app. It is available on Apple and Android smartphones.

Pembrokeshire Coast Path

The Pembrokeshire Coast Path was first established in 1970 and carries National trail status. Stretching for 299km from Amroth in the south to St Dogmaels, the route passes 58 beaches and 14 harbours. It also circumvents attractions such as St Davids, the UK's smallest city and Tenby, a popular seaside resort in Pembrokeshire. The scenery is spectacular and, if walked in its entirety, represents a challenging 11,000m of elevation. The path lies entirely within the Pembrokeshire Coast National Park.

A popular segment of 22.5km will take you from Amroth to Skrinkle (or vice versa). This route passes through Saundersfoot, Tenby and the Blue Flag rated Lydstep beach, with beautiful views of Caldey Island to be enjoyed along the way.

A 19.3km route links Newport to Fishguard, but features a few steep inclines along the way. You can enjoy good views of Ramsey Island on the 20.9km stretch from Whitesands to Solva. View Skomer, Skokholm and Grassholm Islands on the route linking St Martin's Haven to Dale. This section is mostly level, featuring only a brief climb to reach the Dale Plateau.

For less adventurous visitors, there are numerous shorter walks that are nevertheless rewarding. There are good walks of under 2km around Solva, Ceibwr Bay and Abereiddi, while St Martin's Haven, Tenby and Newport also offer easier routes.

Preseli Mountains

While the park consists mainly of coastal areas, it also includes the Preseli Hills, also known as the Preseli Mountains. From this elevated vantage point, you will be able to enjoy spectacular, panoramic views of Pembrokeshire and visit several prehistoric sites. Two ancient quarries in the mountains have been identified as the possible source of the massive boulders that make up Stonehenge.

A great way of exploring this area is by tackling the Golden Road, an 11km trail believed to date back to Neolithic times. The route commences at Bwlch Gwynt, where its first major feature is Foel Eryr or Place of the Eagle, a Bronze Age burial cairn. The path then commences past the Pantmeanog Forest and Foel Cwmcerwyn. As the latter is its highest point, you may want to detour via a footpath to its summit. Continuing, you will encounter more burial cairns - Foel Feddau, Bedd Arthur (according to some legends, a burial place of King Arthur) and Foel Drygarn, an Iron Age fort dated back to 350 BC.

Other notable features are Bwrdd y Brenin also known as the King's Table and Carn Meini. You may also encounter wild ponies, red kite or buzzards along this route.

For a glimpse of ancient history brought back to life, visit Castell Henllys, a re-constructed Iron Age fort. Children can participate in warrior training or view demonstrations of old crafts. There is a Visitor Centre, gift shop, play area and picnic area.

Stackpole Estate & Barafundle Bay

One of the recommended walks in Pembrokeshire explores the area around Bosherston Lakes also known as the Lily Ponds. These are a series of three freshwater lakes that resulted from the flooding of the area's limestone valleys. The lilies are at their best in June and the area is also home to otters, gannets, kingfishers, herons and dragonflies, as well as the indigenous Welsh mountain ponies.

A footpath by the water leads to the beach at Broad Haven South. Broad Haven South and Barafundle Bay form part of the Stackpole Estate, which lies between the villages of Stackpole and Bosherston and is administrated by the National Trust.

Barafundle Bay has been voted the best beach in Britain by the Good Holiday Guide and Country Life. It was once the private beach of the Cawdor Family, who owned Stackpole Estate. There is no road access, but it can be reached via the Pembrokeshire Coast Road, either from Stackpole Quay or Broad Haven South. Stackpole Quay is one of Britain's tiniest harbours and a popular location for kayaking. At low tide, its stony beach area can also be accessed, but beware of being caught by the incoming tide.

Another feature of this route is Eight Arch Bridge, which dates back to the 1790s. Today, it is a great vantage point for observing the otters.

St Govan's Chapel

According to legend, St Govan was nearly captured by Irish pirates, but saved just in time when God revealed a fissure in the cliff. In gratitude, the hermit spent the rest of his days here. Some legends suggest that St Govan was none other than Sir Gawain, one of the nephews (and knights) of King Arthur. St Govan lived in the 6th century, but the tiny chapel dates back to the 13th century. The Bell Rock is believed to contain the saint's silver bell.

The chapel can be accessed by descending a series of steep steps, but therein lies part of the legend. Should you count them, they may not be the same number when you climb back up.

Skomer Island

Skomer Island, also known as Ynys Sgomer, is a must for nature lovers in general and bird watchers in particular. The island is home to a staggering diversity of birdlife, including guillemots, razorbills, great cormorants, black-legged kittiwakes, European storm-petrels, common shags, Eurasian oystercatchers, short-eared owls, common kestrels, peregrine falcons and gulls. In particular, it has the largest breeding colony of Atlantic puffins in the southern part of Britain and significant numbers of Manx shearwaters.

Other wildlife that can be seen include dolphins, porpoises, seals, rabbits and the Skomer vole, a species of land mammal unique to the island. There are signs of prehistoric human settlements and preliminary archaeological exploration has been initiated. In springtime, the island is covered in bluebells.

Be prepared to do a fair amount of walking on uneven terrain, when visiting Skomer Island. Wear comfortable hiking boots and waterproof clothing. Admission is £12 and the boat trip from Martin's Haven to the island is an additional £10. Try to schedule your visit between April and October.

St Dogmaels

St Dogmaels is a picturesque village located at the northern border of Pembrokeshire. One of its most important historical landmarks is St Dogmaels Abbey, which dates back to the 12th century. Next to the abbey, is the church of St Thomas, where visitors can see the Sagranus stone, which bears an inscription in ancient Ogham script, a British alphabet that dates back to the 1st century.

At the Coach House Heritage Centre, you can view an informative presentation on early Celtic inscribed Christian stones - some of which date back as early as the 7th century. The Coach House also hosts exhibitions and craft workshops by local artists.

To the west of the village lies the Blue Flag rated Poppit Sands Beach, the start (or end) of the Pembrokeshire Coast Path. This sandy beach is also a popular spot for paragliding. Just west of the beach is an ancient fish trap, believed to be about 1000 years old. Today it can only be accessed by diving.

Teifi Marsh Nature Reserve

The Teifi Marsh Nature Reserve supports a surprising diversity of wildlife. When the winter flooding occurs, it offers refuge to the region's wildfowl. At various times of the year birdwatchers can see mallards, common teal and swans, as well as moorhens, reed warblers, kingfishers, sparrow hawks and peregrine falcons. The resident water buffalo play a valuable role in maintaining the ecological balance. You can also see Sika deer, red deer, badgers, grass snakes and adders.

Plan your visit by stopping first at the Welsh Wildlife Centre. Here you can get an information pack about its nature trails, including a special geocaching trail. For those just wanting to chill for a while, there is a gift shop, willow maze, adventure playground and picnic areas.

Amroth

The picturesque village of Amroth lies at the southern boundary of Pembrokeshire and its sandy beach marks the beginning (or end) of the Pembrokeshire Coast Path. The beach is the site of a petrified forest which dates back to the most recent Ice Age, but this only becomes visible at low tide. East of the village lies the ruins of Amroth Castle. The Colby Woodland Gardens, which is administered by the National Trust, is another of its attractions.

Fishguard

Fishguard is located in the northern part of Pembrokeshire, where the river Gwaun meets the sea. It may have been a Norse trading post during the 10th century, but today it is best remembered for a more recent historical event. In 1797, the town resisted an invasion attempt by a party of French soldiers, who landed at Carregwastad Point. The pride of the town is a commemorative tapestry which was created for the 200th anniversary in 1997.

Today, the area offers visitors ample opportunity for surfing, kayaking, fishing and horse-riding. There are several scenic walks nearby. Dyffryn Fernant Gardens is the place to go to commune with nature. The garden is gorgeous and filled with abundant, natural vegetation. In a small library area, you can browse through various books on horticulture and (for the price of a modest donation) enjoy hot beverages.

If you like beer tasting tour the Gwaun Valley Brewery. At this family run establishment you can sample the local brews and learn more about the art of beer making.

The Last Invasion Tapestry Gallery

Town Hall,
Market Square
Fishguard, Wales

While the last successful invasion of Britain occurred over 900 years ago, revolutionary French soldiers did attempt to liberate common British folks from their aristocratic rulers in the latter part of the 18th century.

The invasion lasted barely three days, from the landing of a French fleet under Colonel William Tate in Fishguard Bay on the 22nd of February 1797 to its final surrender on the 25th of February. A key figure in rallying the defence was a local woman, Jemima Nicholas, afterwards known as Jemima Fawr or Jemina the Great.

This slice of local history is captured in the Last Invasion Tapestry, a Welsh equivalent of the Bayeux Tapestry. Created with talents and labour of 77 local women and made with over 150 different hues of thread, the tapestry can be viewed in a special room in the town's library, above the Town Hall.

Descriptions are available in Welsh and English and there is a video about the making of the tapestry.

Haverfordwest

The area around Haverfordwest has been settled since the Iron Age, offering the strategic advantage of the lowest fordable point of the Western Cleddau.

An important milestone in its history was when the Normans built Haverfordwest Castle. This imposing structure still towers over the town, although it is mostly a ruin today. To learn more about its history visit the small museum within the grounds.

Today, Haverfordwest is the administrative centre of Pembrokeshire and great place for exploring attractions such as St David and the Pembrokeshire National Park, which are within easy reach.

Picton Castle

http://www.pictoncastle.co.uk/

Picton Castle was built by a Flemish knight in the late 1200s and soon came into the possession of the Wogan family, whose descendants own it to this day.

The castle's garden is particularly noteworthy. Several of the trees are believed to be over 250 years old and an annual highlight is Picton in Bloom, a series of horticultural events that draws visitors to admire its roses, magnolia, camellia and rhododendrons.

The castle frequently hosts raptor encounters in partnership with Pembrokeshire Falconry (http://www.pembrokeshire-falconry.co.uk/), which will enable you to interact with a variety of birds, including owls, hawks, red kites, buzzards and eagles.

Picton Castle is located about 5km east of Haverfordwest.

Oakwood Theme Park

Canaston Bridge, Narberth
Pembrokeshire SA67 8DE
Tel: 01834 815170
http://www.oakwoodthemepark.co.uk/

The Oakwood Theme Park offers adrenaline junkies various opportunities to defy gravity. Vertically accelerate at 70km per hour aboard the Bounce platform or hang from a harness like a human spider with Vertigo. Travel at high speeds when you board the Speed or Megafobia rollercoasters.

Are you brave enough to enter the Spooky 3D Haunted House? Other exciting rides include the Treetops Coaster, the Bobsleigh, the swinging Pirate Ship and Snake River Falls.

There is a boating lake and a mini golf course.

The colourful themed rides at Neverland are for younger visitors and include the Jolly Roger, Skull Rock, the Crocodile Coaster, Hook's House of Havoc and Tink's Flying School. Special nighttime attractions include fireworks and paint powder parties.

You can enjoy meals or light refreshments at the Oakwood Restaurant or the Little Darling Cafe. Facilities for disabled visitors are available. Admission is £24.

Oakwood Theme Park is located in Narberth about 20 minutes' drive east of Haverfordwest.

Blue Lagoon Water Park

Bluestone, Canaston Wood,
Narberth SA67 8DE
Tel: 01834 862410
http://www.bluelagoonwales.com/

The Blue Lagoon is a family-friendly indoor water park located in Narberth and is one of the best places to enjoy a good splash year round. It has a wave pool, water slides, lazy river and a spa pool, as well as a special children's section. The water is heated and there are lounger beds available. Admission is £12.95 per person or £48 for a family ticket. The water park is located within the Bluestone National Park resort.

Milford Haven

Milford Haven is located along the northern bank of the Milford Haven Waterway. As the largest estuary in Wales, it has been used as a natural port since medieval times.

As early as the 9th century, it served as a wintering harbour for a certain Viking chief and both Richard II and Cromwell used it to muster their fleets for the conquest of Ireland. During the 18th century, it served as port for the Nantucket Quaker Whalers. After the construction of an oil refinery in the 1960s, the gas and oil industries played an important role in the local economy.

At the Milford Haven Heritage Maritime Museum, visitors can learn more about the town's proud history in seafaring matters through a series of informative displays. The museum is housed in an 18th century building that once served as a whale oil storage facility. Sailing is a popular pastime and the town has an attractive marina lines with quayside cafes, restaurants and shops.

Dyfed Shire Horse Farm

Carnhuan ,Eglwyswrw,
Crymch, Pembrokeshire, SA41 3SY
Tel: 01239 891 107
http://www.dyfed-shires.co.uk/

The massive Shire horse is one of the largest and strongest of all breeds of draft horses. A pair of two Shire horses are capable of pulling up to 45 tonnes and the largest Shire ever, a 19th century stallion called Mammoth, measured over 21 hands. At Dyfed Shire Horse Farm you will view and learn about these gentle giants.

To get the lay of the land, tour this working farm on a tractor or a horse cart. The highlight of your visit would, of course, be a close and personal encounter with one of the resident Shires, but the farm also has Welsh pigs, Balwen sheep, donkeys and llamas, as well as bunnies, guinea pigs, snakes and giant land snails in the Pet Corner. There is a daily harnessing demonstration. Raptor shows are scheduled on Tuesdays and Thursdays. Additionally, you can also see buttermaking, weaving, donkey grooming and the feeding of baby animals.

Other fun activities include Crazy Golf, croquet, swings, bouncy-castles and play boats. Enjoy a lovely meal at the Caffi Celt.

Admission is £6.95. For budget travellers, the farm has a camping ground where you can stay at £8.00 per night per person. This includes free admission to the farm for the duration of your stay.

The venue can be hired for special events.

Recommendations for the Budget Traveller

Places to Stay

The County Hotel

Salutation Square,
Haverfordwest, SA61 2NB
Tel: 01437 762144

The County Hotel is located in a historical building that dates back to 1842. The bus and train station are located nearby and the hotel has its own free parking. There is free Wi-Fi throughout the building as well as a lounge bar, restaurant and vending machines for drinks and snacks.

Rooms include heating, a kettle and flat screen TV. Free toiletries are supplied. The establishment is pet-friendly. Accommodation begins at £48 and breakfast is included.

White Rose Guest House

Warren Street,
Tenby, SA70 7JT
Tel: 01834 849021
http://www.whiterosetenby.com/

The White Rose Guest House is located in the heart of the popular seaside town of Tenby. It is within easy walking distance of South Beach, harbour, promenade and train station. Rooms are well maintained and comfortable, with flat screen TV, soundproofing and modern ensuite bathroom facilities with hairdryer and complimentary toiletries. Free Wi-Fi is available. Accommodation begins at £60 and includes breakfast.

Lakeland Guesthouse

4 St. Patricks Hill,
Pembroke Dock SA72 6XQ
Tel: 01646 687274
http://www.lakelandguesthouse.co.uk/

Lakeland Guesthouse is located next to the Pembrokeshire Golf Club and within a 10 minute walk from the Pembroke Dock Ferry terminal. Guests can enjoy good views of the river estuary and the decor features a quirky collection of memorabilia and other art.

Rooms are spacious and include a microwave, fridge, tea and coffee making facilities, flat screen TV and ensuite bathroom. Free Wi-Fi and parking is available. Accommodation begins at £40 and includes a Full English breakfast.

Seaview Hotel

Seafront,
Fishguard, SA65 9PL
Tel: 01348 874282
http://fishguardhotel.co.uk/

The Seaview Hotel is situated on the Fishguard seafront and offers stunning views of the ocean and the nearby lighthouse. There is an on-site bar and free Wi-Fi and parking is available. Rooms have flat screen TV and modest bathroom facilities. Accommodation begins at £45 which includes breakfast.

Farmstays in Pembrokeshire

Erw-Lon (http://erwlonfarm.co.uk/) is located in the scenic Gwaun Valley, at the foot of the Preseli Mountains near Fishguard. It is a working sheep and beef farm. There are three rooms available. Each has television, ensuite bathroom and facilities for making coffee and tea.

During your stay, you can enjoy home-cooked meals from local produce. Accommodation is £50 to £55 for single occupancy and £35 to £40 per person sharing. Breakfast is included.

The 18th century farmhouse at Skerryback (http://skerryback.co.uk/) offers close proximity to coastal walking routes and easy access to prime bird watching locations such as Skomer and Skokholm Island. Accommodation begins at £35 and includes breakfast.

Lower Haythog (http://lowerhaythogfarm.co.uk/) is a charming 13th century farmhouse by the village of Spittal, near Haverfordwest. Rooms include television and en suite bathroom amenities and are priced from £35 to £45 per night. Enjoy relaxing walks in its beautiful surroundings. For larger groups, there are two cottages that sleep up to 7 people. These are available at weekly rates.

Langdon Farm (Tel: 01834 814803) in Kilgetty near Saundersfoot is located on a working sheep farm amongst the lily ponds. The location offers easy access to Tenby, Oakwood Theme Park, Folly Farm and the Pembrokeshire Coast National Park. Accommodation begins at £35.

The 17th century Torbant Farmhouse (http://www.torbantfarmhouse.co.uk/) can be found at Croesgoch near St David. It offers modern facilities and the opportunity to observe a large diversity of wildlife nearby. Accommodation begins at £34.

The Dyfed Shire Farm (http://www.dyfed-shires.co.uk/campsite.html) has a camping ground. Pitch your tent at £8 per person.

Places to Eat

The Sound Cafe

18 High Street, St Davids SA62 6SD
Tel: 01437 721717
https://www.facebook.com/The-Sound-Cafe-276058165795467/

The Sound Cafe is a busy eatery located in a charming cottage on High Street in St Davids. Start the day with a full Welsh Breakfast or just settle for a breakfast bab. The jacket potatoes are great for snacks and come in a variety of fillings including baked beans, Welsh mature Cheddar, honey roast ham, tuna mayonnaise and prawns in Marie Rose sauce. There is also a wide selection of toasted sandwiches, including chicken mayonnaise, tuna mayonnaise and Welsh mature Cheddar, with onion, tomato and honey roasted ham. Pizzas come in two different sizes and are priced from £5.75 to £12.25. For burgers, you can choose from lamb, chicken, Angus beef or vegetarian patty. Alternatively just enjoy a refreshing cup of tea or coffee with cake or scones.

Ocean Restaurant

St. Julian's House, St. Julian Street,
Tenby, SA70 7AY
Tel: 01834 844536
http://www.tenby-oceanrestaurant.co.uk/

Ocean Restaurant combines a stylish interior and stunning harbour views with good service and a friendly atmosphere.

Breakfast options range from the budget friendly porridge for £1.50 to the massive Mega Breakfast, a feast of sausage, bacon, eggs, hash brown, beans, mushrooms and toast for £8.50. Also available are muffins, scones, breakfast baps (with bacon or sausage), a Full English and the vegetarian breakfast.

Other options include sandwiches - the Pembrokeshire ham sandwich is a winner - pizza, pasta, omelette, salads and risotto.

For main dishes, try the sea bass or the slow braised Welsh pork belly with smoked bacon, peppers and fresh chilli.

Tenby's Fish & Chips Restaurant

Trafalgar Road,
Tenby SA70 7DN
Tel: 01834 843888

You can find Tenby's Fish and Chips in a quaint little corner shop with indoor and outdoor seating. The house speciality is freshly prepared fish and chips, which is available at £5. The atmosphere is great and service friendly. If your appetite is not too big, try the cone of chips for 99p.

Wavecrest Cafe

West Angle Bay,
Pembroke SA71 5BE
Tel: 01646 641457
http://www.wavecrestangle.co.uk/

The Wavecrest Cafe is located right by the beach overlooking West Angle Bay and offers freshly prepared snacks and meals made from locally sourced ingredients. There is indoor and outdoor seating with beautiful sea views and the service is friendly and efficient.

Enjoy something sweet with your coffee – there is cheesecake, carrot cake, banoffee pie and more to choose from, as well as a range of sandwiches and salads. Favorites include the brie and cranberry melt ciabatta, the coronation chicken sandwich and the crab salad. Check the blackboard for daily specials.

For beverages, try the Elderflower cordial, which is prepared onsite. Expect to pay around £30 for a meal for four. Wavecrest Cafe is open for breakfast and lunch. A roast dinner is served on Sundays.

The Georges Restaurant & Cafe Bar

24 Market Street,
Haverfordwest SA61 1NH
Tel: 01437 766683
http://www.thegeorges.uk.com/

The George Cafe is part restaurant, part coffee shop and part quirky arts cafe. It has a relaxing atmosphere and offers a variety of food choices, including vegetarian and gluten free options. Some of the meal choices are fish chowder, warm goat's cheese salad, beef and Guinness pie, vegetarian lasagne, sea bass and cottage pie.

There is a selection of desserts such as lavender cheesecake, bread and butter pudding, pecan and maple ice cream and sticky toffee pudding. Light meals begin at £6 and desserts start at £4.

Places to Shop

The Sheep Shop

32 Bridge St,
Haverfordwest SA61 2AD
Tel: 01437 766844
http://www.sheepshopwales.co.uk/

If you are looking for an authentic souvenir from Wales, try the Sheep Shop in Haverfordwest. Its signature products are the lovespoons, a beautiful selection of wooden spoons carved with intricate Celtic designs. The custom of giving lovespoons as a token of betrothal dates to the 17th century and different symbols in the design have different meanings.

There is also an adorable range of soft toys - sheep, of course - and for winter you can choose a snug pair of sheepskin gloves or moccasins to keep you warm. For sport lovers, there are Welsh (Cymru) rugby shirts.

On offer is a selection of Celtic jewellery, as well as products of pewter and slate. For edible souvenirs, choose biscuits, fudge, preserves or locally made chocolate. Additionally, the Sheep Shop stocks Welsh beers, wines and spirits.

Wickedly Welsh Chocolate

Withybush Trading Estate
Withybush Road,
Haverfordwest SA62 4BS
Tel: 01437 557122
http://wickedlywelsh.co.uk/

The Wickedly Welsh Chocolate Company offers visitors the chance to learn more through chocolate making demonstrations and an informative talk on the history of chocolate. If you want to try what you learnt, use the opportunity to craft your own lolly or chocolate pizza. There is a range of hot chocolate drinks to sample on site. Chocolate is sold by the slice or you can also choose from the wide selection of bars or truffles. Wickedly Welsh is located on the outskirts of Haverfordwest.

The Nook

St Julian's Street, Boro House,
Tenby SA70 7AS
Tel: 01834 844078
http://www.thenooktenby.co.uk/

The Nook showcases the work from 60 different Welsh artists and crafters, offering visitors the opportunity to take a little part of Pembrokeshire home with them. There are a wide variety of products including ceramics, textiles, children's clothing, candles and even decorative hooks and doorknobs. One range of wooden products is made from reclaimed wood. If you are a fan of visual media, you will also be able to choose from a selection of art and photographic prints.

Felin Fach Handmade Textiles

Yr Hen Felin, Blaenffos,
Boncath, Pembrokeshire, SA37 0JA
Tel: 07599 640 997
https://www.felinfach.com/

Felin Fach is located in Blaenffos in the heart of the Preseli Mountains within the Preseli Coast National Park and stocks a beautiful variety of local wool products.

The range includes scarves, handmade cushions, organic blankets, Welsh tapestry blankets, throws, purses and spectacle cases. Most of the wares are made from sheep or lamb's wool, but a limited number of alpaca products are also available. Felin Fach is partnered with Campaign for Wool, an initiative to promote Welsh wool products.

Shopping in Narberth

The town of Narberth offers good shopping opportunities for its visitors. Start with a leisurely stroll on the High Street. The Welsh Farmhouse Company sells a selection of quirky country living products. Visit the Golden Sheaf Gallery or No. 47, if you are looking for craft items. Pay a visit to Narberth Pottery to see the range of ceramics. If you like beading visit Begelly Bead Shop for supplies. Susie's Sheepskin Boots will keep your feet warm and if you like vintage and retro fashion, go to Giddy Aunt on Market Square. Foodies can sample artisan ice creams at Fire and Ice.

Printed in Great Britain
by Amazon